DECREMENT INDICES

Purpose, Performance, Pricing, Hedging, Marketing.

ERIC BARTHE

DECREMENT INDICES

*"Wise people learn when they can,
fools learn when they must."*

Arthur Wellesley,
First Duke of Wellington

TABLE OF CONTENTS

ABOUT THE AUTHOR

Eric Barthe has traded, designed, analyzed, researched and taught structured products and exotic derivatives for the last 20 years

He was an equity exotics trader at Goldman Sachs in London for 8 years, trading Index exotics, single stock exotics and dispersion. He was managing director at Leonteq Securities as global head of financial engineering. He taught finance at HEC Paris Business School and EDHEC Business School.

He holds a Master of Science from the London School of Economics in Finance & Economics, from Ecole Centrale Paris in Engineering and from HEC Paris in Management.

He regularly holds seminars for industry professionals and created a "Derivatives Bootcamp" for students aspiring to join investment banks.

You can follow his activity on www.structuredproducts.net

INTRODUCTION

In recent years, decrement indices have captured substantial interest from retail investors, accumulating significant volumes. Attracted by their distinctive structure that offers the potential for higher yields along with certain protective features, these instruments have become a favored option for those in pursuit of enhanced returns. Introduced in the mid-2010s, decrement indices are tailor-made for use as the underlying assets in structured products, particularly autocallables. Throughout the rest of this book, I will primarily use the term "Decrement Index." However, it's important to note that decrement stocks function in the same way as decrement indices but have a single stock as the underlying asset instead of an equity index.

Decrement indices were created to simultaneously achieve two objectives:

- They enhance the appeal of structured products by offering higher coupons and/or lower barriers, which is advantageous for the end investors.
- They significantly mitigate the risks faced by trading desks when hedging these products, which benefits banks.

However, decrement indices differ fundamentally from conventional equity indices. They hold distinct economic significance, and their expected returns are also different. For the end investors and their wealth advisors, it is crucial to understand how they are constructed, what sets them apart from regular equity indices, and what their performance relative to regular equity indices is expected to be. For structurers and traders, it is key to understand how they can be hedged and priced.

In this booklet, I will make an effort to minimise the use of mathematics unless it adds value, ensuring accessibility to a broad audience, including investors, wealth managers, sales professionals, structurers, and traders. Occasionally, mathematical concepts may be necessary, but I will strive not to lose sight of the underlying intuition behind the formulas.

This book will be divided into three parts. In the first part, I will refresh the reader's understanding of the dividend risk typically borne by banks when they sell structured products. Next, I will explore the dividend market and its dynamics. Finally, I will delve into the world of decrement indices.

DIVIDEND RISK IN STRUCTURED PRODUCTS

Decrement indices were developed to eliminate the dividend risk accumulated in the trading books when issuing structured products based on standard indices. Therefore, it is essential to understand these risks from the outset.

When it comes to the risks they present to a trading desk, it's important to recognise that not all structured products are the same. As expected, the more complex a structured product is, the more complex the associated risks become. I will now review the most common yield enhancement structured products to emphasise the type of dividend risk they involve.

Reverse Convertibles

The simplest yield enhancement products, like reverse convertibles, are theoretically perfectly hedgeable. This is because the bank's synthetic position essentially involves being long a vanilla put (*as shown in Figure 1*). If the traders can locate the same strike and maturity date in the market, they can simply sell it, achieving a perfect hedge from day one until maturity. No additional rehedging will be necessary throughout the life of the reverse convertible except for potential upsizes and downsizes.

However, in practice, there is typically some degree of mismatch, resulting in some residual dividend risk, even with those straight-forward yield enhancement products.

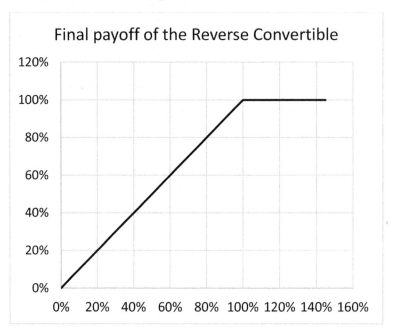

Figure 1: Final payoff (excluding coupons) of a Reverse Convertible as a function of the final spot level vs initial level. The investor is implicitly short a put, usually at-the-money or a levered out-of-the-money put. The bank is implicitly long that vanilla put.

Barrier Reverse Convertibles

Let's explore the second class of yield enhancement products: the barrier reverse convertible.

I'll begin by discussing the European barrier. From the bank's perspective, the payout can be over-hedged by combining the sale of a narrow put spread with a put (see Figure 2).

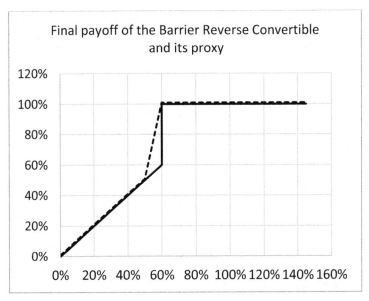

Figure 2: Final payoff (excluding coupons) of a Barrier Reverse Convertible as a function of the final spot level vs initial level. Here, the barrier is 60%. The investor is implicitly short a down-and-in put represented as a plain line. The bank is implicitly long that down-and-in put, which can be overhedged by selling a tight put spread and a put in a dotted line.

In theory, once again, there should be no dividend risk as the hedge could be established on day one and wouldn't require rebalancing until maturity. In practice, it's challenging to perfectly match maturities and strikes. Moreover, implementing such a hedge would be prohibitively expensive in terms of bid/ask spreads due to the high leverage of the narrow put spread. Consequently, banks typically avoid employing this expensive hedge and, instead, focus on hedging the vega and skew risk by selling an out-of-the-money (OTM) Put. To eliminate any dividend risk at the outset, an additional forward trade is used.

If, at a later point, the market experiences a downturn, two effects manifest in the trader's book: the long digital put augments the short forward position, while the short put (sold as a hedge) increases the long forward position. However, the influence stemming from the digital put is more pronounced (the delta of a digital put considerably increases as the spot approaches the strike). Consequently, as the market declines, the bank becomes net short on forwards or long on dividends, a position that is less than ideal since dividends tend to decrease when the market goes down. To maintain a balanced hedge, the bank must sell dividends, making it imperative to accurately predict future dividend prices.

Conversely, when the market rises, the short put used for hedging introduces more risks than the digital put, and the bank ends up being net short on dividends. To retain a balanced hedge, the bank must buy dividends, again necessitating an accurate prediction of future dividend prices.

When the barrier is continuous, the necessity of dynamic hedging is even more pronounced. Indeed, when the barrier is crossed, the product instantaneously transforms itself into a vanilla put without barrier, and the digital risk disappears. So, the digital hedge needs to be unwound. The price of unwinding that hedge will depend on where the implied dividend will be at the hitting time, which also needs proper modelling.

Autocallable Barrier Reverse Convertibles

The Autocallable Barrier Reverse Convertible introduces a dimension of duration to the risk dynamics of the Barrier Reverse

Convertible. To illustrate this, let's consider a 2-year autocallable product that can autocall in the first year if the underlying asset's value exceeds 100% of its initial value, with a final barrier at 60%. Without the autocallable feature, as we've discussed previously, there is already a dynamic related to dividend risk. However, the auto-callable feature further complicates this dynamic, as outlined below:

Imagine you're in the situation the day after the strike date. Assuming a 50% probability of autocalling, you can reasonably assume that the dividend risk is 50% of the risk associated with a standard BRC. When the underlying asset's value decreases, two simultaneous events occur:

- The probability of not autocalling increases, meaning there's a greater chance for the trader to hold the BRC until maturity.
- The dividend risk stemming from the final BRC increases for the reasons explained in the previous section.

As a trader, you end up with a riskier position due to the compound effects of these two factors. This amplification of dividend risk is more pronounced than in the case of a fixed maturity BRC.

When the market moves upward, the effects are exactly the opposite. However, they still compound: The trader ends up with a less risky position and will need to adjust his dividend hedge accordingly.

The dynamics described above highlight the importance of having a model that accurately predicts how dividends will behave as the market moves.

When the market shifts, the trader's dividend exposure increases or decreases, necessitating adjustments to the hedge. The model is crucial in forecasting at what price these adjustments can be made. If the model is inaccurate, unexpected gains or losses may occur. While one outcome is certainly preferred over the other, it is essential for the model to closely approximate reality. Let's now explore some dividend models.

DIVIDEND MODELS

Before discussing the desirable features of a dividend model, it's worth revisiting what traditional valuation models tell us. Equity valuation models establish a connection between dividends and equity value: the price of a stock is equivalent to the sum of the discounted expected dividend stream. This means that if all dividends are adjusted 10% higher, the equity price should also be adjusted higher by 10%, assuming all else remains equal. This observation supports the idea of a so-called fully proportional model, where stock price and dividends should move in a one-to-one relationship.

However, history reveals that companies tend to maintain relatively stable dividend payments over time, with some growth in absolute amounts to make their stock an attractive investment for investors. Furthermore, dividends expected to be paid in the near future are largely based on past earnings. They should not fluctuate in tandem with the stock price.

In practice, dividend models often strike a balance between these two approaches by making the initial dividends somewhat stable (typically in the first year) and making dividends in the distant future fully proportional (typically over a 5-year period). For the interim years, dividends exhibit a combination of stickiness and proportionality.

The models described above primarily factor in changes in dividends due to market movements. Some more advanced models might assign their own volatility to dividends. But that topic is beyond the scope of this discussion.

Example

Let's consider a hypothetical scenario: Today, the index is valued at $1,000, and the prevailing interest rates are at zero. The market is currently pricing the 1-year dividend at $30 (as implied by the one-year forward) and forecasts dividends at $30 for the second year, $28 for the third year, $27 for the fourth year, and $26 for the fifth year. Consequently, the 5-year forward is valued at $1,000 - $30 - $30 - $28 - $27 - $26, which sums up to $859.

Now, let's compare the dynamics of the forward according to three distinct models:

Model 1

Fully Sticky

In this model, dividends remain constant. So, if the index experiences a sharp decline of 10% (equivalent to $100), Model 1 predicts that all dividends will remain unchanged. Consequently, the new forward would be calculated as follows: $900 - $30 - $30 - $28 - $27 - $26, resulting in a new forward value of $759. In this case, the forward drops by the same amount as the index. If a trader is short $100 million of forwards (perhaps through structured products), they will make $11.6 million, implying that they should be long $116 million of the index to remain hedged.

Model 2

Hybrid

This model incorporates a combination of sticky and proportional dividends. For instance, the 1-year dividend is fully sticky, while the 2-year dividend is 50% sticky and 50% proportional. From the 3rd year onward, dividends are fully proportional. When the index experiences a 10% decline, the new forward would be calculated as follows: $900 - $27 - $28.5 - $28 - $27 - $26, resulting in a new forward value of $763.5. In this scenario, the forward drops by only $95.5. Consequently, the short forward position generates $11.1 million. Model 2 indicates that the trader should carry only $111 million of the index to remain hedged.

Model 3

Fully Proportional

In this model, all dividends move in direct proportion to the index. So, when the index experiences a 10% decline, the new forward is calculated as follows: $900 - $27 - $27 - $25.2 - $24.3 - $23.4, resulting in a new forward value of $773.1. Here, the forward drops by only $85.9, generating $10 million for the short forward position. According to Model 3, the trader needs to be long $100 million of the index to remain properly hedged.

This simple example demonstrates the critical role of selecting the right model for hedging. Suppose the trader uses Model 1, but the dividends actually behave in a fully proportional manner. In that case, the trader's hedge will be excessively long by $16 million, leading to a loss of $1.6 million with a 10% index decline.

When dealing with positions that are not merely $100 million but extend to several tens of billions, the implications of such model choices become even more pronounced, as witnessed in the tumultuous financial landscape of 2020

DIVIDEND MARKETS AND THE ROUT OF 2020

Reminder about economics

So far, our discussion has centered on dividends as a fundamental pricing parameter of the underlying forward. However, it's important to recognise that the payment of dividends is a corporate decision, subject to a specific calendar. Typically, at the outset of each year, often in January or February, a company's board of directors convenes to review the previous year's financial results, denoted as year N-1. Based on those results, the board proposes the amount of dividends to be paid in year N. These dividend payments can occur quarterly, semi-annually, or annually.

The proposal made by the board doesn't immediately become a finalised dividend; it undergoes a formal process. Subsequently, it needs to be voted upon at the Annual General Meeting (AGM), where shareholders typically convene in the spring. After the AGM, the dividend becomes official and is known for the entirety of year N. This finalised dividend amount is determined based on the financial results of year N-1.

It's worth noting that it is quite rare for a dividend policy proposed by the board to not receive approval at the AGM. Shareholders often endorse the board's recommendation, making the dividend amount official.

Dividend markets

Dividend futures, along with their over-the-counter (OTC) equivalents known as dividend swaps, provide traders with a means to speculate on or hedge dividend payments related to indices or individual stocks.

Consider a 2028 Euro Stoxx 50 dividend future, which has a set expiration in December 2028. The settlement value of this future is calculated as the sum of dividends paid by the constituents of the Euro Stoxx 50 index from the third Friday of December 2027 (exclusive) to the third Friday of December 2028 (inclusive). This means that as early as, say, 2025, a trader can engage in trading a December 2028 Euro Stoxx 50 dividend future to take a position or hedge against dividends that will be disbursed between December 2027 and December 2028.

In recent developments, semi-annual dividend futures have been introduced on Eurex, allowing traders to focus on dividends paid between December N and June N+1.

The life and dynamics of a dividend future vary significantly depending on whether its expiration is several years, just a couple of years, or mere months away. Broadly, the life of a dividend future can be divided into three key phases, using a 2028 dividend future as an example:

Early Life: In the years leading up to 2027, the 2028 dividend future is closely tied to the market's movements, moving more or less in a one-to-one relationship.

For instance, in 2024, it's too early for analysts to confidently predict dividend payments for the year 2028. As a result, the dynamics of the dividend future are influenced by market flows and conditions.

Year N-1: During 2027, the companies constituting the index will provide interim financial results. As the year progresses, the uncertainty regarding the financial results for 2027 gradually diminishes. This decrease in uncertainty translates to reduced volatility in the 2028 dividend future.

Year N: At the onset of 2028, companies will publish their full-year financial results for 2027, along with proposed dividend amounts. At this stage, almost all uncertainty is eliminated. The primary risk for the dividend is the possibility that the Annual General Meeting (AGM), held in the spring, might reject the proposed dividends or introduce new dividend proposals for unforeseen reasons. Historically, this risk is quite remote. However, in 2020, due to regulatory and governmental pressures resulting from the COVID lockdowns, companies had to adapt their initial dividend payment plans to align with the public subsidies they were receiving. This risk is only magnified in instances where a company defaults and fails to make its dividend payments. As 2028 unfolds, dividends are actually disbursed, and the 2028 dividend future gradually stabilises, converging toward its final settlement value (*as shown in Figure 3*).

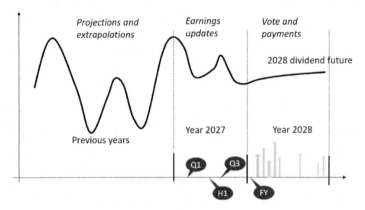

Figure 3: The three stages of the life of the Dec 2028 dividend future. The first phase is where the 2028 dividend moves in line with the overall market. Then, in the year 2027, financial results become the basis for the 2028 dividend level. Uncertainty decreases as financial results are released, and the dividend becomes less volatile. At the beginning of 2028, full-year results for 2027 are published, and the dividend levels are proposed and subsequently voted upon at the AGM.

Term structure and dynamics

Now that we have a grasp of the life cycle of dividend futures, it's straightforward to understand the dynamics of the term structure of dividends. A term structure essentially provides a snapshot at time "t" of all the dividend futures, each of which is at a different stage of its life.

The front end of the dividend futures curve comprises contracts in the latter stages of their life. Their value is influenced primarily by microeconomic fundamentals and the expected dividend payments for the upcoming one or two years. This segment of the curve exhibits a low beta, or sensitivity, to broader market movements.

On the other hand, the back end of the term structure is influenced by the spot market and the flow, primarily driven by structured products used for hedging. This portion often moves in near lockstep with the overall market, with a beta close to one.

As traders sell long-term dividend futures to hedge against structured product flows, the term structure of dividends typically exhibits a state of backwardation. In other words, long-term dividend futures are trading at a discount when compared to the historical average of dividends. Consequently, when an investor purchases a yield enhancement product, they effectively sell future dividends at a lower price than those dividends have historically averaged. This highlights that the investor is synthetically selling future dividends too cheaply compared to their historical norms.

Maturity	Futures price	Implied dividend yield
2023	143.1	3.46%
2024	149.2	3.61%
2025	140.5	3.40%
2026	134.4	3.25%
2027	129.5	3.13%
2028	125.0	3.02%
2029	122.2	2.95%
2030	121.7	2.94%

Figure 4: The Euro Stoxx 50 dividend term structure as of 13 October 2023 (source eurex.com). The 2023 dividend has mostly been paid, so it is not moving anymore. The 2024 value is mostly based on the 2023 intermediary earnings revealed so far. The rest of the curve is mainly the structured products desks selling dividend futures to hedge their risks; hence, the downward sloping structure with 2030 quoting at only a 2.94% dividend yield when 2024 is around 3.61%.

The 2020 rout

The pivotal year for the evolution of decrement indices was 2020. The surge in the distribution of Decrement Indices can be attributed to the fact that hedging conventional indices became prohibitively expensive for the major players.

To fully comprehend the implications of 2020, it's crucial to understand why it was such a challenging year for trading desks. Many players openly disclosed massive losses related to dividends within their structured product portfolios. While there hasn't been an official disclosure of the total losses, estimates based on the hardest-hit players suggest the losses could exceed $2 billion industry-wide. What exactly happened?

Let's go back in time. 2019 saw robust global economic growth. In early 2020, companies announced their annual results for 2019, and their boards recommended dividends. By early February, for the Eurostoxx, the 2020 dividend value was nearly certain. Traders treated this dividend as a settled figure.

The European market reached its zenith in late February, only to plummet by 35% within weeks due to the onset of COVID-19. Concurrently, long-term dividends also declined in tandem with the broader market.

As the equity market deteriorated, dividend exposure intensified in trading books, a phenomenon previously explained. However, traders weren't initially concerned, as their models accounted for the parallel movement of long-term dividends with the market. Surprisingly, the 2021 dividend mirrored the market's every move, likely leading to some losses as 2021 was modelled as partially sticky. Yet, the 2020 dividend remained steady, as anticipated.

However, the situation worsened in March 2020. Governments instituted lockdowns, halting international flights and jeopardising the global economy. The European Systemic Risk Board (ESRB) advised banks to withhold 2020 dividends due to the pandemic and to reserve capital for potential losses and loan provisions. Simultaneously, governments, while offering financial aid to companies, encouraged businesses to withhold 2020 dividends. This blend of economic downturn and regulatory directives drastically altered the trajectory for 2020 dividends. Despite earlier board recommendations, these dividends faced uncertainty, causing the futures for 2020 dividends to plummet.

While the market depreciated by 35%, the 2020 and 2021 dividends slumped by up to 60%. This outcome defied traders' models; even a model predicting proportional behaviour wouldn't have forecasted such a drop. Consequently, traders were forced to offload surplus 2020 dividend exposure at a 60% markdown and surplus 2021 dividend exposure at a 43% reduction relative to their models. Moreover, the 2022 and 2023 dividends also dropped more than predicted. In March and April 2020, amidst a 35% downturn in European markets, banks were compelled to reduce their dividend exposure, solidifying most of the losses.

In April 2020, notable companies like LVMH, L'Oreal, and Royal Dutch Shell adjusted or completely withdrew their dividend proposals. The total loss in dividend payments globally approximated $200 billion, as reported by Janus Henderson, with Europe, the UK, and Asia Pacific (excluding Japan) being the most affected regions.

By June 2020, the 2020 dividends had moderately recuperated, ending the year at a 33% deficit compared to 2019. Given the vast losses reported that year, it's unsurprising that banks subsequently began championing decrement indices over traditional indices.

Now that the stage is set, let me introduce Decrement Indices!

DECREMENT INDICES

What are decrement indices?

Standard equity indices typically measure price returns.

However, some measure total returns. A total return index accounts for dividends, usually after taxes, and assumes their reinvestment back into the index. In essence, it showcases the value of holding the stocks component of the index over time, taking into account received dividends and their reinvestment. A prominent example of such an index is Germany's DAX 30 Index.

In contrast, price return indices exclude dividends. They can be perceived as a version of the total return index wherein the dividend is not considered. Consequently, the trajectory of a price return index does not mirror the wealth progression of an investor who possesses a portfolio comprising the index's components. For instance, if the Euro Stoxx 50 stands at 4,000 now, an investor would spend €4,000 to purchase one unit of that portfolio. If, a year later, the Euro Stoxx 50 climbs to 4,400, the investor's gains would be 400 euros per unit plus the dividends received during that period, say 120 euros. So, even though the Euro Stoxx index reflects a value of 4,400, the investor's actual wealth amounts to 4,520. The price return index reports a gain of 10%, while the total return portrays a 13% increase. Thus, the price return index trails the total return index by the dividend's value. Mathematically: Return of Price Return Index = Return of Total Return Index - Dividend contribution.

While the 4,400 level doesn't depict the investor's wealth, it does indicate the amount an investor must spend to acquire one unit of the index a year later. Consequently, the total and price return variations of an index bear economic significance, albeit for different reasons.

Distinctly, a decrement index is a synthetic construct. It takes a total return index as a base and deducts some dividends, which are predetermined or "synthetic." This predetermined dividend is termed the "decrement", "contractual dividend", "decrement fee" etc. Unlike standard dividends, which are often distributed biannually or quarterly, this synthetic dividend is disbursed continuously, usually on a daily basis. The decrement can be a specified percentage (commonly around five percent) or an absolute number of points. Thus, every day, the decrement index will deviate from the total return index by the daily decrement's magnitude. It will also deviate from the price return index based on the discrepancy between the decrement and the actual dividend.

Unlike a total or price return index, a decrement index has no economic meaning as the decrement is (often) set to a level unrelated to the underlying index's real dividends. The level of the decrement index does not reflect the wealth of someone invested in the market or the price to enter that market.

In the rest of the booklet, I will refer to three different types of indices:

- *The Underlying Index (I will note it I)*: by definition, it is the index that serves as a base for constructing the decrement index. It is most often a net total return index.

For instance, the Eurostoxx 50 net total return or the CAC 40 net total return. It can also be a customised basket of shares, net total return. Theoretically, it could also be any self-financed trading strategy on any asset class (a systematic volatility strategy on equity, a CTA on commodities, a static basket of shares with reinvested dividends, a dynamic multi-asset allocation, etc.).

- *The Decrement Index (I will note it as S^*):* By definition, it is a synthetic index built iteratively every day from the daily performance of the Underlying Index but modified by a Decrement. The formula is explicitly shown in the index documents.

- *The Standard Index (I will note it as S):* This is the way I will call the standard price return index, for instance, the regular Euro Stoxx 50, CAC40, or S&P500. This is the most common and liquid index, on which futures and options are usually the most liquid in the listed or OTC markets.

Percentage Decrement vs. Fixed Points Decrement

There are two types of decrements: percentage decrements and fixed-point decrements. While it might not seem immediately apparent, the distinction is significant. My aim for this section is to ensure the reader grasps the difference between those two. I will note $S^{*\%}$ as the percentage decrement Index and S^{*pts} as the fixed-point decrement index.

Percentage decrement

Any decrement index (S^*) has a start date, an initial value (generally 1000), and an underlying index (I) from which it is derived. From its initial value, S^* is then computed daily by applying:

- The return of the underlying I
- The discount due to the decrement D, which is applied according to a day-count convention

Let's take two consecutive business days, t and t+1, and call DC(t,t+1) the number of calendar days between t and t+1 (it will generally be 1, except for weekends or bank holidays), assume the day-count convention is Act/365, then:

$$S_{t+1}^{*\%} = S_t^{*\%}\left(\frac{I_{t+1}}{I_t} - D * \frac{DC(t, t+1)}{365}\right)$$

Where D is the decrement in percentage (typically 4% or 5% nowadays).

From that definition, a small amount is taken away from the "true" return of the Underlying Index. Unlike with standard indices or even more so with stocks, dividends here are not detached discreetly on the ex-dividend dates but every day, almost continuously. With a stock, there is always a risk that the company changes the time it pays dividends or how often it pays dividends. With percentage decrement, the synthetic dividend yield is known, and the payment dates (every day) are also known, so two risks are actually erased from the trading books simultaneously!

Let's take an example. On Friday, the Decrement Index is worth 1000. Assume the return from Friday to Monday of the Underlying Index (net total return) is -6.00%. What is the return of the corresponding decrement index 5% ACT/365?

Here, DC = 3 D=5%, so the return is -6% - 5%*3/365= -6.04%. The decrement index will then be worth 939.59.

Assume the Underlying Index is down another -6% from Monday to Tuesday, then the return of the decrement index is -6% - 5%*1/365 = -6.01%. The decrement will then go down from 939.59 to 883.09.

Note that in the previous computations, if you know the return of the Underlying Index, you can deduce the return of the Decrement Index. It is true for a Percentage Decrement but not for a fixed-point Decrement, as we will see later.

Note also that if the convention were ACT/360, the return would be slightly lower… it is always important to check the details! Different providers may use different conventions.

Back of the envelope, the annual performance of the 5% decrement will lag by 5% per annum behind the Underlying Index (net total return). We also know that if the Standard Index has a realised dividend yield of 3%, it will lag 3% per annum behind the Underlying Index. Consequently, in that case, the 5% Decrement Index will underperform the Standard index by 2% per annum.

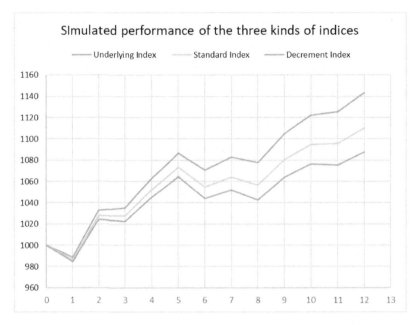

Figure 5 : Simulated performance of the Underlying Index, the corresponding Standard Index with a dividend yield of 3% and a Decrement Index of 5% month after month.

Over a span of 7 years, the 5% Decrement Index will underperform the Standard Index by -13% (calculated as (1+(3%-5%))^7-1). Put differently, in 7 years, a barrier of 60% for the 5% Decrement Index is roughly equivalent to a barrier of 69% for the Standard Index. Unsurprisingly, everything else held constant, barriers are lower on Decrement Indices than on Standard Indices. It is simple mechanics…

Fixed points decrement

When the decrement is specified in terms of index points rather than as a percentage, a fixed number of points are subtracted from the Underlying Index instead of a proportional amount. This point-based decrement is predetermined, and its level is recursively determined by the following formula:

$$S_{t+1}^{*pts} = S_t^{*pts} \frac{I_{t+1}}{I_t} - D * \frac{DC(t, t+1)}{365}$$

Where D is the number of points (typically 40 or 50 points for an index starting at 1000).

Example:

On Friday, the Decrement Index is worth 1000. Assume the return from Friday to Monday of the Underlying Index (net total return) is -6.00%. What is the return of the corresponding decrement index 50 points ACT/365?

Here, DC = 3 D=50 points, the decrement index will be worth 1000*0.94 – 50*3/365 = 939.59.

Assuming the Underlying Index is down another -6% from Monday to Tuesday, the new value of the decrement index will be 939.59*0.94-50*1/365= 883.08.

Again, note that if the convention was ACT/360, the return would be a touch lower.

As a rough estimate, if both indices start at 1,000 points, the yearly performance of the decrement, compared to the performance of the Underlying Index (net total return), will be 50 points lower. Whereas the underperformance in points is easy to estimate, the underperformance in percentage is not easy to forecast. Indeed, if the Underlying Index goes up to 2000 points, then the fixed-points Decrement Index will still underperform by 50 points, which is only

2.50%. On the other hand, in a bear market where the Underlying Index goes to 500, the fixed-points Decrement will underperform by 50 points, which is then 10%. On the other hand, in both scenarios, the Percentage Decrement Index will underperform by 5%. In other words, the fixed-point decrement will outperform on the upside and underperform on the downside.

It's also worth noting that nothing prevents the fixed-point decrement index from becoming negative. Often overlooked by many investors, this nuance also has significant implications on the trading side.

In Figure 6, I plot three scenarios where the market (with dividend reinvested) is always flat, up 5% or down 5% yearly. For each of those scenarios, I also plot the performance of a Standard Index with a 3% dividend yield, a 5% Decrement Index, and a 50-point Decrement Index using the iterative formulae described earlier.

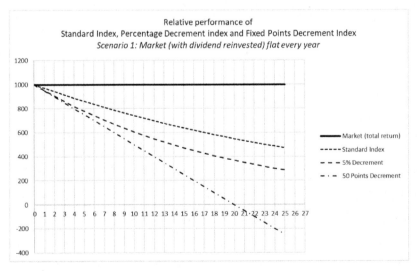

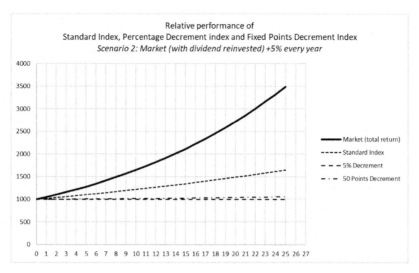

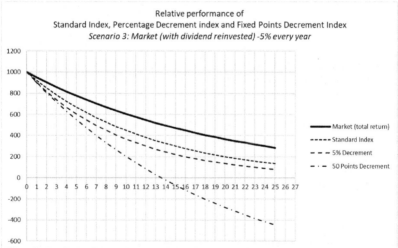

Figure 6: Relative performance of a 3% dividend yield Standard Index, a 5% Decrement Index and a 50 points Decrement Index in three scenarios for the Underlying Index: flat every year, up +5% every year, down -5% every year.

Additionally, when I compared percentage and fixed-point decrement, I assumed they were initially at the same level (1000). Hence, 5% and 50 points are initially "equivalent." But if a fixed decrement quotes at 900, its 50 fixed point decrement will be equivalent to a 50/900=5.55% decrement. That is also what the graphs above say: the more the market goes down, the heavier the fixed decrement weights on the index's performance, hence the important underperformance in scenarios 1 and 3.

Now that the reader has a good grasp of the two types of Decrement Indices and how they relate to the Underlying Index and the Standard Index, I will dive deeper and try to price options on them.

PRICING AND HEDGING

In this section, I will try to describe in more detail how the spot level of the Decrement Index is related to the spot level of the Underlying Index, allowing me to think about the forward and implied volatility of the synthetic decrement index.

This section will first address the percentage decrement index, then the fixed decrement index.

Percentage decrement

To price derivatives on the Decrement Index, let's go back to its definition. Usually, the Decrement Index is defined by

- An initial value is given to the index (usually 1000) on a specific initial date.
- Then, the value of the index on the next day is defined iteratively by the following formula:

$$S_{t+1}^{*\%} = S_t^{*\%} \left(\frac{I_{t+1}}{I_t} - D * \frac{DC(t, t+1)}{365} \right)$$

Where D is the percentage decrement.

It can be rewritten as:

$$\frac{S_{t+1}^{*\%}}{S_t^{*\%}} - 1 = \frac{I_{t+1}}{I_t} - 1 - D * \frac{DC(t, t+1)}{365}$$

In simpler terms, every day, the return of the Decrement Index is equal to the return of the Underlying index from which some kind of percentage decrement fee is deducted. As a consequence, with a percentage decrement of 5%, if after 2 years the Underlying Index is up 7%, the Decrement Index return after 2 years will be

$$(1 + 7\%) * (1 - 5\%)^2 - 1 = -3.4\%$$

Assuming the Standard Index has a dividend yield of 3%, the Standard Index's return will be

$$(1 + 7\%) * (1 - 3\%)^2 - 1 = +0.6\%$$

Buying (or selling) a 2-year option with a strike at 107% on the Underlying Index should be equivalent to buying (or selling) a 2-year option with a strike at 96.6% on the Decrement Index and equivalent to buying (or selling) a 2-year option with a strike at 100.6% on the Standard Index. This implies that the implied volatility for these three indices at those specific strikes should be the same. Therefore, if you have access to the volatility surface data for the Underlying Index or the Standard Index, you can easily deduce the implied volatility for the Percentage Decrement Index.

Let's show that result more rigourously for readers familiar with financial mathematics. Switching to continuous time and calling δ the continuous proportional decrement, you have:

$$\frac{dS_t^{*\%}}{S_t^{*\%}} = \frac{dI_t}{I_t} - \delta \, dt$$

And by integration :

$$S^{*\%}(T) = S^{*\%}(0) * \frac{I(T)}{I(0)} e^{-\delta T}$$

That equation is very intuitive and is the continuous version of our previous numerical examples. We see here with this formula that the underperformance of the Decrement Index over the Underlying Index is easy to compute and does not depend on the path taken by the Underlying Index, only its final performance. Whatever the performance of the Underlying Index is, one just needs to multiply it by $e^{-\delta T}$ to get the performance of the Decrement Index.

The equation above allows us to compute easily the forward of the decrement index :

$$\mathbb{E}_o^Q[S^{*\%}(T)] = S^{*\%}(0)e^{(r-\delta)T}$$

δ being known, there is no dividend risk left in the forward of the Decrement Index. Job done!

Let's now take a look at options on the decrement index. For that purpose, let's simply consider a call option on the decrement index, maturity T, and strike K:

$$Max\left(0,\frac{S^{*\%}(T)}{S^{*\%}(0)} - K\right) = Max\left(0,\frac{I(T)}{I(0)}e^{-\delta T} - K\right)$$
$$= e^{-\delta T}Max\left(0,\frac{I(T)}{I(0)} - Ke^{\delta T}\right)$$

Calling $BSC(S,K,\sigma_S(K))$ the Black-Scholes price of the call option, the equality above means that at any time :

$$BSC\big(S,K,\sigma_{S*}(K)\big) = e^{-\delta T}BSC\left(I,Ke^{\delta T},\sigma_I\big(Ke^{\delta T}\big)\right)$$

Where σ_{S*} is the implied vol of the decrement index, and σ_I is the implied volatility of the underlying index.

But the Black-Scholes price has the well-known property of being homogenous:

$$BSC(\lambda S, \lambda K, \sigma) = \lambda\, BSC(S,K,\sigma)$$

So, the right-hand side can be rewritten :

$$BSC\left(S, K, \sigma_{S*}(K)\right) = BSC\left(Ie^{-\delta T}, K, \sigma_I\left(Ke^{\delta T}\right)\right)$$

$$BSC\left(S, K, \sigma_{S*}(K)\right) = BSC\left(S, K, \sigma_I\left(Ke^{\delta T}\right)\right)$$

We have

$$\sigma_{S*}(K) = \sigma_I\left(Ke^{\delta T}\right)$$

That equation allows us to price options on the percentage decrement index if we can access options on the Underlying Index. More and more indices now have total return futures and options, so the Underlying Index has, indeed, an option market. In that case, the trader who is long a put strike K on the Decrement Index will sell a put strike $Ke^{\delta T}$ on the Underlying Index.

Suppose there are no options on the Underlying Index. In that case, traders will have to hedge using options on the corresponding Standard return index that we call S. If one calls div_yield the implied dividend yield of the price return index S, it is easy to reproduce the same reasoning as above and conclude that:

$$\sigma_{S*}(K) = \sigma_S\left(Ke^{(\delta - div\_yield)T}\right)$$

In that case, the trader who is long a put strike K on the Decrement Index will sell a put strike $Ke^{(\delta - div\_yield)T}$ on the Standard Index. We see here that the term div_yield is present in the strike of the Standard Index. So if div_yield changes, the trader will not be hedged on the correct strike anymore. Let's take an example:

Imagine the trader wants to hedge his 5-year exposure on a 5% decrement Index using a Standard Index with a 3% implied dividend yield. This is the implied volatility surface of the Standard Index for 5-year options :

Strike	88.41%	92.95%	97.71%
Volatility	28.12%	27.05%	26.36%

What is the implied volatility of the Decrement Index at strike 80%? The previous result tells us that it should be the same as the volatility of the Standard index at strike $80\% \; e^{5(5\%-3\%)} = 88.41\%$. So the volatility strike 80% of the decrement Index is 28.12%. Imagine the trader then puts the hedge on; he will be long the 80% put on the Decrement Index and short the 88.41% out on the Standard Index, both with the same volatility.

Now imagine that the dividend yield of the Standard Index goes down to 2%, then the volatility of the Decrement Index should be remarked down to 27.05% $(80\% \; e^{5(5\%-2\%)} = 92.95\%)$. So the trader loses on his long leg (that goes from 28.12% to 27.05% volatility) and does not make it on the short leg: he loses money when the dividend yield goes down.. he is then long dividends because of the volatility skew of the Standard Index.

Fixed points decrement

We already mentioned that it is not trivial to infer the return of the Fixed Points Decrement Index when you know the return of the Standard Index. A priori, it is only possible to say that the fixed point decrement will be, say, 50 points lower per year. But looking at the definition, it looks like things are a bit more complicated. You have the following iterative definition:

$$S_{t+1}^{*pts} = S_t^{*pts} \frac{I_{t+1}}{I_t} - D * \frac{DC(t, t+1)}{365}$$

For the sake of simplicity, we assume that the day count is always 1 (there is no weekend or bank holiday!) and call d the daily fixed decrement. Then we have:

$$S_{t+1}^{*pts} = S_t^{*pts} \frac{I_{t+1}}{I_t} - d$$

By iteration,

$$S_T^{*pts} = S_0^{*pts} \frac{I_T}{I_0} - d * I_T \sum_{t=1}^{T} \frac{1}{I_t}$$

That last equation demonstrates that it is not enough to know the performance of the underlying index to know the performance of the fixed points decrement index. Indeed, you can see that the last term imposes the knowledge of the values of I_t from time 1 to T to compute S_T^{*pts}. In other words, the final value of the fixed point decrement at time T depends on the path of the underlying index from time 0 to T! It is a major difference from the proportional decrement.

To fix ideas, let us take an example below where two paths for I lead to the same final value of I_T but not to the same value for S_T^{*pts}. To magnify the effect, I take the decrement to be 3 points at each date. Both paths 1 and 2 start at 1000 and go back to 1000. Path 1 first goes up and then falls back. Path 2, on the contrary, first falls before going back to 1000. For each path scenario, the value of the Decrement Index is computed, and one can see that they do not end up at the same value.

Date	Path 1 for I	Decrement	Path 2 for I	Decrement
0	1000	1000	1000	1000
1	1050	1047.00	995	992.00
2	1100	1093.86	990	984.02
3	1200	1190.30	985	976.05
4	1150	1137.70	975	963.14
5	1050	1035.77	978	963.10
6	1020	1003.18	987	968.96
7	1000	**980.51**	1000	**978.73**

So we can say two things: given that the decrement is 3 points per day, the best initial guess is that the decrement index will end up 21 points below the Underlying Index. So, if you want to hedge the 800 strike on the Decrement Index, you should hedge the 821 strike on the Underlying Index. But as the market evolves, you want to readjust that hedge. Indeed, if the market first goes up, you expect the difference to be less than 21 points (say 20..), so you should unwind your 821 strike hedge and hedge now with the 820 strike. On the contrary, if the market first goes down, the 819 strike hedge may have to be put in place. In other words, hedging a vanilla option on the Fixed Decrement Index needs a dynamic hedging strategy using options on the Underlying Index.

Moreover, as we already saw, nothing prevents the fixed point Decrement Index from becoming negative. Imagine that the Underlying Index is not moving at all; a 50-point decrement index, starting at 1000, will be down 50% after 10 years and become negative after 20 years.

The formula giving the final value of S_T^{*pts} is not trivial. Nevertheless, its forward is not so complex. We can switch to continuous time, for instance, and write:

$$S_T^{*pts} = S_0^{*pts} \frac{I_T}{I_0} - d \int_0^T \frac{I_T}{I_u} du$$

$$\mathbb{E}_o^Q[S_T^{*pts}] = S_0^{*pts} e^{rT} - d \int_0^T e^{r(T-u)} du$$

Which can be rewritten as:

$$\mathbb{E}_o^Q[S_T^{*pts}] = S_0^{*pts} e^{rT} - \frac{d}{r}(e^{rT} - 1)$$

We can easily compare the forward of a proportional decrement index and a fixed points decrement index.

Proportional decrement : $\mathbb{E}_o^Q[S_T^{*\%}] = S_0^{*\%} e^{(r-\delta)T}$

Fixed point decrement : $\mathbb{E}_o^Q[S_T^{*pts}] = S_0^{*pts} e^{rT} - \frac{d}{r}(e^{rT} - 1)$

The two formulas generate the exact same forwards at all maturities if

$$r = \delta = \frac{d}{S_0^*}$$

That result is actually quite intuitive. When that equality holds, in expectation, both percentage and fixed point decrements stay constant at their initial value. If r is lower, then the Underlying Index is not increasing enough in expectation. So, the low paths prevail, and the fixed point decrement has a lower forward than the percentage decrement.

With an interest rate of 5%, a 5% percentage decrement will have the same forward as 50 points decrement starting at 1000. If interest rates are lower, then the fixed points decrement will have a lower forward.

To exhibit the path dependency, let's now look at the forward at time t (knowing that at time 0, both Decrement Indices started at 1000):

It is trivial to show that for the Percentage Decrement :
$$\mathbb{E}_t^Q[S_T^{*\%}] = S_t^{*\%} e^{(r-\delta)(T-t)}$$

The ratio Forward over Spot is then : $\dfrac{\mathbb{E}_t^Q[S_T^{*\%}]}{S_t^{*\%}} = e^{(r-\delta)(T-t)}$

For the fixed point decrement, write:

$$S_T^{*pts} = S_t^{*pts}\frac{I_T}{I_t} - d \int_t^T \frac{I_T}{I_u} du$$

Taking expectations as of time t:

$$\mathbb{E}_t^Q[S_T^{*pts}] = S_t^{*pts}\frac{\mathbb{E}_t^Q[I_T]}{I_t} - d \int_t^T \mathbb{E}_t^Q\left[\frac{I_T}{I_u}\right] du$$

$$\mathbb{E}_t^Q[S_T^{*pts}] = S_0^{*pts}\frac{I_t e^{r(T-t)}}{I_0} - \frac{d}{r}(e^{r(T-t)} - 1$$

If we look at the ratio:

$$\frac{\mathbb{E}_t^Q[S_T^{*pts}]}{S_t^{*pts}} = \frac{S_0^{*pts}}{S_t^{*pts}} \frac{I_t e^{r(T-t)}}{I_0} - \frac{d}{S_t^{*pts} r}(e^{r(T-t)} - 1)$$

The ratio is made of 2 components:

- A total return component stating that forward should grow at r
- A decrement adjustment that is all the higher as S_t^{*pts} is lower.

Here, we retrieve the intuition that the forward is really hit when S_t^{*pts} is low. It is of particular importance where the driver of the pricing is not the simple forward but rather the conditional forward. That is typically the case of autocalls where what matters is the forward of the index subject to it being below the autocallable triggers. If the index goes up, the product will auto-call, so there is no damage. If the index goes down, the fixed point decrements will hit both the spot and the forward more importantly than a percentage dividend. That is why the coupon offered by a fixed point decrement is higher than a percentage decrement.

To quantify those remarks, I ran some basic simulations. I simulate an Underlying Index with a 2.70% return per annum (it is the average total return of European markets over the last 20 years) and a 25% constant volatility. I construct the 5% decrement and the 50 points decrement using tnat Underlying Index and look at the final distribution of the three indices after 7 years. Results are plotted in figure 7 . The results confirm that the expected value of the 5% decrement and the 50 points are comparable.

I then restrict myself to paths where the Underlying index ends at 70% (precisely between 698 and 702)

With not surprise, the expected value of the percentage decrement Index has an expected value of 493 (indeed 700 * 0.95^7 is around that level). But the expected value of the 50 points decrement is only 397 with a wide standard deviation. Most likely, if the Underlying Index ends at 70% after 7 years, it means that the Standard index will end at 56% (assuming 3% dividend yield) it means that the 5% decrement will end up at 49% and that the 50 points decrement will end up at 40%.

Nonetheless the uncertainty on the actual outcome for the 50 points decrement is significant due to the path dependency. See Figure 8.

Finally, I plot the distribution of both kinds of Decrement Indices after 7 years, subject on those indices being below 1000 after 1 year, after 2 years,..., after 6 years. In other words, I look at the expected value of both indices, assuming there was no autocallable event. It is an important graph to look at when you are an investor at that is ultimately what will determine if your capital is reimbursed at maturity or not. I plot the results in Figure 9.

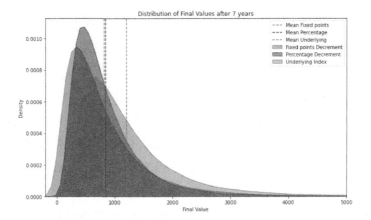

Figure 7 : Distribution of final values of the Underlying index, the 5% Decrement Index and the 50 points Decrement Index assuming all start at 1000 and 25% volatility for the Underlying Index. Although the means are similar for the Percentage and the Fixed points, the distribution of the Fixed Points Decrement is more skewed. In particular, the probability of the Fixed points decrement being negative is non null.

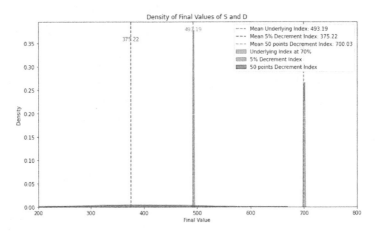

Figure 8 : Distribution of final values of the 5% Decrement Index and the 50 points Decrement Index assuming all start at 1000 and 25%

volatility for the Underlying Index, and subject to the Underlying index ending up at 70%. Note how the skewed distribution of the 50 points Decrement Index kicks in now with an expected value of only 397.03 versus 493.20 for the 5% decrement Index. Also note how uncertain the final outcome for the 50 points Decrement Index is, indeed there are many paths for the Underlying Index that leads to 700. All those paths roughly lead to 493.20 for the 5% Decrement Index. But each of those paths have a very different outcome for the 50 Points Decrement, which translates into a wide probability distribution.

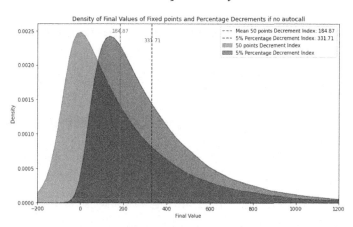

Figure 9 : Distribution of final values of the 5% Decrement Index and the 50 points Decrement Index assuming all start at 1000 and 25% volatility for the Underlying Index, and subject to the the Decrement Indices being below 1000 at each annual observation. The reader may be surprised to see how low the means are. Indeed, under those conditions, the 5% Decrement Index has an expected value of 331.71 while the 50 points Decrement Index has an expected value of 184.87 (only). The reader will also note the high probability that the 50 points Decrement Index end up in negative territory.

Now that we understand better the forward of the fixed point decrements, let us have a look at the implied volatility. For that purpose, let's just write the payoff of such an option:

$$Max\left(0, \frac{S^*(T)}{S^*(0)} - K\right) = Max\left(0, \frac{I_T}{I_0} - \frac{d}{S_0^*}\int_0^T \frac{I_T}{I_t}dt - K\right)$$

The payout above is not a vanilla option on the Underlying Index. The integral is, in fact, the sum of forward starting returns. So, that exotic option is a variation of cliquet options. No static replication of that option is possible even if the trader has access to all options on the Underlying Index. The trader will need a stochastic volatility model to correctly price forward start volatility and the dynamics spot/vol on the Underlying Index to retrieve the implied volatility of the decrement Index.

Remember that the fixed point Decrement Index can take negative values, so implicitly, the investor is actually not short a put or a down-and-in put on that Index but rather a put spread or a down-and-in put spread where the higher strike is usually 100%, and the lower strike 0%. For ease of explanation, let us assume that there is no barrier in the structured product we are considering and that the investor is implicitly short a 100%/0% put spread on the Decrement Index. Assume the maturity is 5 years.

The trader is then implicitly long that put spread. Even though we have seen no static replication possible, we can get some intuition of the hedge the trader should put in place on the first day. Assume the Decrement Index is at 1000 and the decrement amount is 50. Assume the Underlying Index also quotes at 1000 and has an option market. Assume a flat interest rate curve at 3%.

Using the formulae we derived, and since both indices are assumed to start at 1000 on the strike date, we know that the forward of the Decrement Index is lower than the forward of the Underlying Index by an amount equal to:

$$\frac{d}{r}(e^{rT} - 1) = 269.7 \; points$$

As a first guess, the 0/1000 put spread on the Decrement Index is initially equivalent to a 269.7/1269.7 put spread on the Underlying Index. That is the initial hedge the trader should put in place. Note here that sourcing a 27% strike put is not easy for the trader as those very low strikes are rarely liquid, and people tend not to sell those very out-of-the-money options. Unfortunately for the trader, he is implicitly short that very out-of-the-money puts, so he better buy it somehow to control his crash scenarios.

If the market then goes down, the path dependency that we highlighted means that the trader should adjust the strikes of the put spread that he sold. The very nature of the fixed decrement implies some dynamic hedging. On top of that, one needs to add the inherent dynamics of the autocallable itself. Combining both, when the market goes down, two things happen :

- The probability of autocalling decreases, to the probability that the trader will end up long the put spread on the Decrement Index increases, so the trader should sell more put spreads.
- The path dependency of the fixed Decrement Index kicks in, and the strikes of the hedges need to be adjusted down.

Use Case in Capital Protected Notes

While our focus has primarily been on yield enhancement products, it's worth noting that Decrement Indices can also serve as an underlying for capital-protected structures. When structuring capital protected notes, it is all about creating cheap call options. As discussed earlier, the percentage decrement typically exceeds the implied dividend yield of the Standard Index, resulting in a lower forward value for the Decrement Index. Simultaneously, at the same moneyness level, the implied volatility of the Decrement Index tends to be lower. For call options, in contrast to puts, both the lower forward value and decreased volatility contribute to making the option more cost-effective when written on a Decrement Index.

We have also seen that the Fixed Point decrements are more complex and less effective on the upside. You are then less likely to see Fixed Point Decrement Indices in Capital Protected Notes; percentage Decrement Indices will generally be the choice of banks.

At this point, it's evident to the reader that while dividend risk has been addressed, the volatility risk is still present in the trading books. Banks often implement volatility control mechanisms to mitigate this risk: they leverage the Underlying during periods of low volatility and deleverage it during periods of higher volatility so the resulting volatility remains close to a target volatility. Predicting the future performance of such products becomes highly challenging when the Underlying of the call option is an Equity Index with a volatility target and decrement.

On the other hand, with no dividend risk and minimal volatility risk, it becomes possible to use virtually any index as the Underlying

Index. This index doesn't need to have an option market; it can encompass a wide range of assets, including systematic trading strategies on equities, fixed income, options, cross-asset baskets, long/short commodities ir any self-financed strategy you may imagine.

HOW ARE THEY CREATED AND MARKETED?

We have shown that decrement indices remove a substantial part of the risks in the investment banks' books, especially the Percentage Decrement Index. Their advantages for the banks are clear. But for them to be attractive for the investors too, they also need to offer the following:

- Better terms (higher coupons or lower barrier or both) than standard indices: standard indices are still offered by some banks, so the terms offered by decrements need to be more attractive.
- A compelling past performance versus standard indices
- The expectation of a future good performance.

Better Terms

Suppose the long-term implied dividend yields are approximately 3%, as depicted in Figure 4. In that case, the Decrement Index needs to have a yield of 4% to 5% to present a more favorable picture. This is especially important considering the loss of implied volatility discussed earlier. The put (or down-and-in put) on the Decrement Index is more expensive because the decrement level is higher than the implied dividend (a dominant effect). However, it's also cheaper due to its lower implied volatility, assuming the Underlying Index exhibits a volatility smile, where low strikes have higher volatilities than high strikes.

It's worth noting that the price impact of the Decrement Index becomes more significant for maturities of 5 years or longer. For shorter maturities, Decrement Indices don't necessarily offer better optics.

Past performance

If the standard index historically had a yield of 3% (as is the case with Euro Stoxx 50, for example), the Eurostoxx 50 with a 5% decrement would exhibit a historical underperformance of 2% compared to its benchmark. The more favorable terms offered by the Decrement Index might persuade investors to choose it.

However, it's important to note that banks typically don't use a standard index in its total return version as the underlying index. Instead, they often create "new" indices to set themselves apart from the competition.

On the other hand, these "new" indices can't be entirely novel. Decrement indices effectively eliminate most of the dividend risk but do not eliminate the volatility risk. In the case of fixed points, they even introduce some additive stochastic volatility risks and very low strike risk. Consequently, banks need to select underlying indices that are not too different from standard indices, allowing them to hedge the volatility risk on the decrement index by selling volatility on the standard index.

As a result, the underlying index of the decrement index will be a slight variation of a standard index. For example:

Equal weighting

It's a common practice to use the equally weighted version of a standard index as the underlying for a decrement index, and this serves two primary purposes.

First, historically, though it's less pronounced nowadays, small-cap stocks have tended to outperform large-cap stocks. Equally weighted indices would typically outperform market-cap weighted indices. Using an equally weighted index as the underlying can bring about some outperformance that can partially offset the under-performance generated by the decrement mechanism.

Secondly, an equally weighted index is generally more volatile than a market-cap-weighted index. As a result, traders can buy volatility on a more volatile asset and may offer this to clients in the form of a higher coupon or lower barrier. The equal-weighted feature is often denoted in the name of the decrement index by the letters "EW."

Thematic filtering

Instead of using the exact same weights as the standard index, the underlying index could slightly overweight stocks that, for instance, have a strong ESG score or exhibit attributes that align with the thematic goals the bank aims to promote, such as decarbon-ization, water conservation, exposure to specific economies, geo-graphies, or technologies, or risk factors like value, among others.

By strategically overweighting factors or themes that have historically outperformed, one could construct a decrement index with a strong track record of performance compared to the standard index. Will those factors continue to excel in future markets?

Future performance

When historical performance fails to persuade, the strategic design and titling of the decrement index play a pivotal role in projecting the potential of future returns. This is where strategically chosen nomenclature, infused with compelling buzzwords such as "growth", "green", "champions", "ESG", "artificial intelligence", "leaders", "future leaders" etc. steps in to capture investor interest. These terms are not mere catchphrases; they suggest a forward-looking, thematic investment approach that may resonate with an investor's personal outlook and market predictions.

The promise of future performance anchored in such a thematic selection has the potential to be more than just marketing gloss. When well-executed, it can reflect a genuine convergence of the index's strategy with emergent market trends and sectors poised for expansion. This alignment can offer a tailored investment vehicle that truly embodies the theme it purports to represent, setting it apart from the conventional offerings in the market.

Nevertheless, due diligence is paramount. Investors need to peel back the layers of attractive terminology to verify that the index's composition is authentically aligned with its thematic label. This involves scrutinizing the underlying assets, the selection criteria, and the index's methodology to confirm that they collectively work towards the espoused theme. The caution here is that a thematic label should not serve as a veneer for an index that, upon closer inspection, reveals itself to be a mere tweak of a standard benchmark. Such superficial labeling could mislead investors seeking thematic exposure and dilute the value of genuinely thematic indices in the marketplace.

CONCLUSION

Decrement indices have gained significant popularity in Europe, especially in countries like France, Germany, and Italy. They are likely to increase their market presence in other regions where long-dated Index autocallables are in demand. Therefore, it is essential for all stakeholders, including investors, financial advisors, wealth managers, structurers, and traders, to grasp their dynamics.

As the reader is aware by now, Percentage decrease indices effectively eliminate dividend risk, provided that the total return Underlying Index itself has an option market. It's no surprise then that the option market for total return indices and futures is evolving. Fixed Point Decrement Indices can be more intricate in terms of hedging. However, the development of an option market for total return indices is equally valuable for them.

Like most financial innovations, Decrement Indices come with both benefits and risks. The removal of risks for investment banks is advantageous for all parties involved, as everyone shares an interest in banks avoiding losses. In this regard, Percentage Decrements are generally more benign than Fixed Points. However, it's crucial for investors, financial advisors, and wealth managers to have a clear understanding of the complex behavior and expected performance trajectory of these new indices.

This booklet aimed to shed light on the reasons for their development, their anticipated performance compared to conventional benchmarks, their marketing strategies, and provide insight into the pricing and hedging of these instruments. It also aimed to highlight the risks that are mitigated and the risks that are introduced. I hope that by doing so, I've contributed to a better understanding of these innovative indices, which are playing a significant role in the retail investment market.